TV **COOKS**

Sophie Grigson

COOKS

Vegetables

Photographs by Philip Webb

BBC BOOKS

Published by BBC Books,
an imprint of BBC Worldwide Publishing.
BBC Worldwide Limited, Woodlands,
80 Wood Lane, London W12 0TT.

The recipes in this book first appeared in:
Eat Your Greens
© Sophie Grigson 1993
Sophie Grigson's Travels à la Carte
© Sophie Grigson and William Black 1994

We would like to thank Channel 4 for allowing
us to adapt recipes from **Eat Your Greens** and
Sophie Grigson's Travels à la Carte.

The television programmes **Eat Your Greens**
and **Sophie Grigson's Travels à la Carte**
were produced by Wall to Wall Television and
Antelope West respectively for Channel 4.

This edition first published 1997
© Sophie Grigson 1997
The moral right of the author
has been asserted

ISBN 0 563 38345 3

Edited by Pam Mallender
Designed by DW Design
Photographs by Philip Webb
Stylist: Helen Payne
Home Economist: Annie Nichols
Author photograph by Sandra Lane

Set in New Caledonia and Helvetica
Printed and bound in France by Imprimerie Pollina s.a.
Colour separations by Radstock Reproductions Limited,
Midsomer Norton
Cover printed in France by Imprimerie Pollina s.a.

Cover and frontispiece: Asparagus and Gruyère Quiche

CONTENTS

RECIPE NOTES

Eggs are large (formerly size 2). Spoon measurements are rounded, unless otherwise stated.

Never mix metric or imperial measures in one recipe. Stick to one or the other. (You will find some ingredient conversions do not match the tables below. There is no need to be concerned. The recipes have been tested using both imperial and metric weights and will work perfectly if you follow just one set of measurements.)

Wash all fresh produce before preparation and peel as necessary.

Vegetables do not come in standard sizes, so in some instances you will have to use your own judgement as to, say, how large a large aubergine is, or how long it will take the pumpkin you've bought to cook. Where no specific size or weight is stated, assume that it means an average or medium-sized specimen.

Cooking times are there as guidelines only, so don't rely absolutely on my 15 minutes or whatever. Check for yourself and allow a few less or a few extra minutes if necessary.

Taste as you cook wherever possible, and adjust flavourings to your liking. I happen to be particularly fond of garlic, chilli and fresh herbs. It's up to you to decide whether your taste for these ingredients matches mine. You may prefer your food less or more highly seasoned.

HANDY CONVERSION TABLES

Weight		Volume		Linear		
15g	½oz	30ml	1fl oz	5mm	¼in	
25g	1oz	50ml	2fl oz	10mm/1cm	½in	
40g	1½oz	100ml	3½fl oz	2cm	¾in	
55g	2oz	125ml	4fl oz	2.5cm	1in	
85g	3oz	150ml	5fl oz (¼ pint)	5cm	2in	
115g	4oz	175ml	6fl oz	7.5cm	3in	
140g	5oz	200ml	7fl oz (⅓ pint)	10cm	4in	
175g	6oz	225ml	8fl oz	13cm	5in	
200g	7oz	250ml	9fl oz	15cm	6in	
225g	8oz	300ml	10fl oz (½ pint)	18cm	7in	
250g	9oz	350ml	12fl oz	20cm	8in	
280g	10oz	400ml	14fl oz	23cm	9in	
350g	12oz	425ml	15fl oz (¾ pint)	25cm	10in	
375g	13oz	450ml	16fl oz	28cm	11in	
400g	14oz	500ml	18fl oz	30cm	12in	
425g	15oz	600ml	20fl oz (1 pint)			
450g	1lb	700ml	1¼ pints	**Oven temperatures**		
550g	1¼lb	850ml	1½ pints	225F	110C	GAS ¼
750g	1lb 10oz	1 litre	1¾ pints	250F	120C	GAS ½
900g	2lb	1.2 litres	2 pints	275F	140C	GAS 1
1kg	2¼lb	1.3 litres	2¼ pints	300F	150C	GAS 2
1.3kg	3lb	1.4 litres	2½ pints	325F	160C	GAS 3
1.8kg	4lb	1.7 litres	3 pints	350F	180C	GAS 4
2.25kg	5lb	2 litres	3½ pints	375F	190C	GAS 5
		2.5 litres	4½ pints	400F	200C	GAS 6
				425F	220C	GAS 7
				450F	230C	GAS 8
				475F	240C	GAS 9

(f) **Low fat**   ✳ **Suitable for freezing**

Vegetables are wonderful things, far more interesting in every way than meat. Quite why they get relegated time and again to second place is a bit of a mystery to me. Perhaps it is because they are, relatively speaking, cheap and commonplace. Common they may be but they nonetheless steal the show when it comes to looks. The ample curve of an onion, the fire-red glow of a ripe tomato, the elegant tapering form of a spring carrot, topped with a marvellous feathery display of green, pearly young turnips or the crinkled, dark green leaves of a Savoy cabbage – truly beautiful sights if only we bothered to pause and take time to admire them.

Pause and take time to consider their flavours and textures, too, before you cook your vegetables. Simply cooked – just steamed or lightly boiled or fried as appropriate – they will be good enough as a side dish, but it doesn't take much more effort to bring out their superlative qualities, transforming them into veritable feasts that will give immense pleasure to even the most ardent carnivore. Indeed, if you accord vegetables a little respect and prepare them with love, you may soon find that you eat them in preference to meat, reversing the old-fashioned notion of 'meat and two veg', to produce the more modern 'vegetables with a side order of meat', or even no meat at all. Far more interesting, far more varied, far healthier, far more satisfying, far more fun, and probably far cheaper into the bargain!

INGREDIENTS

Asparagus

Whatever its girth asparagus, or 'grass' as it is known in growing circles, should be firm and smooth (no tired wrinkles) and sprightly green, with no slimy patches marring its beauty. The tips should be tightly packed. Tips that are opening belong to elderly asparagus, picked past its best. Cook and eat as soon as possible after buying.

Aubergines

Although you can cook aubergines just as they are, you will be well advised to salt them first. Salt draws out (or dégorges) some of their juices and improves the flavour. Unsalted aubergines may have what is usually described as a bitter flavour, though that's not really quite the right word. It's more tinny than bitter, an aftertaste rather than an upfront impression. Salted aubergines will absorb less oil when they are fried, a bonus, both calorie- and pocket-wise. They also develop a more voluptuous texture.

Carrots

Very young carrots need little preparation other than a good wash to rinse off the dirt. As they get older and bigger, they may need to be scraped and eventually, at full size, peeled. Look out in the shops for 'baby carrots' (actually fully mature carrots of a miniature variety) and the little, round, extra-sweet Paris carrots, more highly priced than usual, but worth splashing out on from time to time.

Celery

When it comes to buying celery, it always seems obvious to me that it should be fresh and firm, though all too often I've seen it for sale in a state of depressed limpness, stems patched with brown, and the fine head of leaves shorn off as if it were of no interest. The leaves have a powerful but delicious flavour, and can be used as a herb in soups or sauces, or chopped fresh into salads or cream cheese. To prepare celery for the table, separate the stalks and trim off dry ends. Pull off any strings down the outside. Stand in a jug of iced water, or place in a plastic bag with a sprinkling of water, knot the bag to seal it and keep in the vegetable drawer of the fridge.

Chicory

Good chicory is firm and unblemished with yellow rather than green or browning edges to the leaves. The chicons should be tightly packed, tapering neatly to a point. Sometimes you may have no choice but to buy ones with some bruising on the outer leaves. As long as the damage is not extensive, they can be stripped off. Store chicory in brown paper in the bottom of the fridge, where it will keep for four or five days. Radicchio is a red, unforced chicory that grows green until the cold weather sets in triggering the transformation to dark purple-red streaked with white.

Fennel

Fennel is not cheap to buy so choose it carefully to minimize waste, and remind yourself that a little stretches a long way. Size is of no importance: big fat bulbs are usually just as juicy and tender as more slender ones. The condition of the vegetable is what counts. Look for firm, ivory orbs, with no soft or browning patches. The tufts of feathery green fronds should still be bright and fresh. If the fennel is in good condition when it enters your kitchen, it will keep for around four days or even longer.

Garlic

Like onions and shallots, most of the garlic that we buy has been 'cured' or semi-dried. The individual cloves are still juicy (or at least they should be) but enough moisture has been dried off from the outer layers of skin to keep the garlic firm for months on end. There is now a brief season, usually in late June, for 'green' or 'wet' garlic. These newly pulled, undried heads of garlic have large cloves and are delightfully juicy. Their taste is a little fresher and livelier than cured garlic, but there is not a massive difference. If you do use 'wet' garlic you will be surprised to discover that it takes longer to cook.

Globe artichokes

These vary in shape and size from squat, tightly packed balls to looser-leaved tapering ones, according to variety. Choose them carefully, discarding any that seem dry or elderly. The leaves and stalk should be fleshy with no tell-tale brown patches.

Jerusalem artichokes

One thing is certain about Jerusalem artichokes; they have nothing whatsoever to do with Jerusalem, nor for that matter with artichokes proper. They come, in fact, from North America where they have long been a staple of native North Americans. The Cherokees call them *gu-ge* and still use them to make relishes, while the traditional way of cooking was to roast them in the embers like baked potatoes.

Olive oil

When I use olive oil it is always extra virgin olive oil, a blended commercial brand for general cooking and a classier, more highly flavoured single-estate olive oil for salads and as a condiment at the end of cooking. Plain olive oil, which used to be known as 'pure olive oil', has a milder flavour and you may prefer it for general use. Wherever I think the stronger taste of extra virgin oil is essential, I've listed it specifically in the ingredients.

Paprika

This is merely dried, finely ground, mild red peppers (as in capsicums not peppercorns). However, that is by no means the end of the story. Spanish paprika, which is mildly smoky, is markedly different from the Hungarian variety, with more of a metallic tinge; not surprisingly as they are ground from different cultivars. Unfortunately most of the paprika sold in this country is anonymous, and we just have to use what we can get. However, Spanish delicatessens may stock proper Spanish paprika (*pimentón*).

Parmesan

Never ever buy this ready grated in little tubs. It's vile stuff, stale and old and stinky. Parmesan should always be bought in a piece and grated when needed. You'll be amazed by the difference. Store hunks of Parmesan wrapped in foil in the fridge, but open them up once every couple of days for a quick breath of fresh air.

Parsnips

Opt for middled-size roots harvested before the fibres become tough and stringy and the core too woody. Only with enormous parsnips should you bother to remove the core – more easily done when partially cooked.

Peppers

There's a veritable rainbow of peppers to be had these days. Besides red and green, there's yellow, orange and dark, black-purple-skinned types. Occasionally the pale green, conical banana or Hungarian wax pepper puts in an appearance, too. In flavour they boil down to a choice of two. Green ones have a more savoury taste – not so surprising as they are merely unripened red (or yellow or orange) peppers. Fully ripened red, orange and yellow ones are sweeter. The remarkable purple peppers are a bit of a disappointment; the moment you cook them the brooding colour fades to a murky green. Save them for a bit of dark drama in a salad. Never buy peppers that are wrinkled with damp, squishy patches. They are well past their sell-by date.

1 Creamed horseradish

2 Pumpkin

3 Parsley

4 Fresh broad beans

5 Baby beetroot

6 Beetroot

7 Asparagus

8 Globe artichokes

9 Aubergine

10 Florence fennel

11 Baby carrots

12 Courgettes

13 Red onions

14 Small turnips

15 Jerusalem artichokes

16 Large turnips

17 Whole heads of garlic

18 Celery sticks

19 White chicory head

20 Red chicory head

21 Fresh chives

22 Tuna steaks

23 Fresh chervil

24 Whole nutmegs

25 Cooking chorizo

26 Black pudding

27 Parmesan

28 Poussins

29 Flaked almonds

30 Pine nuts

31 Dill seeds

32 Fennel seeds

33 Caraway seeds

34 Frozen broad beans

Soups

GAZPACHO

Gazpacho, the 'liquid salad', is a soup I never tire of. Once on a visit to Spain, I was shown an old wooden bowl for making gazpacho, smoothed and sculpted through years of pounding. Pounding it by hand is a long tedious job, but with a food processor preparing it is a matter of minutes.

Serves 6

675g/1½lb ripe, richly flavoured tomatoes, skinned, seeded and roughly chopped

¾ cucumber, peeled and roughly chopped

1 large green pepper, seeded and roughly chopped

½ red onion, chopped

2–2½ tbsp red wine vinegar

5 tbsp olive oil

115g/4oz fresh white breadcrumbs

2 garlic cloves, roughly chopped (optional)

½–1 tsp sugar

salt and freshly ground black pepper

ANY OR ALL OF THE FOLLOWING GARNISHES

diced, seeded tomato

diced cucumber

diced red onion

diced green pepper

diced *jamón serrano* (Spanish air-dried ham)

1 Place all the ingredients in a food processor with a small slurp of iced water. Process to a fairly smooth sludge (you may have to do this in two batches if your processor bowl is small).

2 Gradually stir in enough water to give a soupy consistency, 300–425ml/ ½–¾ pint should do it. Taste and adjust the seasoning, adding a little more salt, vinegar or sugar as necessary to highlight the flavours.

3 Chill, and adjust the seasoning again just before serving. Place the garnishes in small bowls and pass around for people to help themselves.

Nutrition notes per serving: *162 calories, Protein 3g, Carbohydrate 16g, Fat 10g, Saturated fat 1g, Fibre 2g, Added sugar 1g, Salt 0.45g.*

TIP

Remember that the proportions of vegetables and other ingredients given in the recipe are there merely to serve as a starting-point. Tomatoes, peppers, garlic, etc. will vary in flavour from one batch to another, so it's important to keep tasting and to adjust the seasonings to compensate for any inadequacies. To intensify both the tomato flavour and colour of the soup you can replace some of the water with tomato juice, or add a tablespoon or two of tomato purée.

POTATO AND KALE SOUP

When visiting a market in Portugal, I was fascinated by the shredding machines that sat on many of the vegetable and fruit stalls. In front of each drum was a heap of finely shredded vegetables for soup – more often than not threads of *couve*, a green-leaved cabbage, used to make *caldo verde*, Portugal's favourite soup. The nearest thing to *couve* that I've found here is curly kale, sturdy and dark, but spring greens, or Savoy cabbage make fine alternatives.

Serves 4

450g/1lb potatoes, sliced

1 garlic clove, sliced

½ small onion, finely chopped

salt and freshly ground black pepper

225g/8oz curly kale

115g/4oz *chouriço* or Spanish *chorizo*, sliced

4 tbsp extra virgin olive oil

1 Place the potatoes in a large pan with the garlic, onion, salt and pepper and enough water to cover generously. Simmer until tender. Pass through the fine blade of a mouli-légumes, or mash to a smooth purée. Add a little more water, if necessary, to thin to a soupy consistency. Return to the pan, taste and adjust the seasoning, adding plenty of pepper.

2 Cut the stalks from the kale, then roll up the leaves and shred very thinly (the resulting threads of cabbage should be around 3mm/⅛in wide).

3 Bring the soup back to the boil. Stir in the kale and sausage and simmer for 5 minutes. Ladle into bowls and pour a tablespoon of olive oil into each one.

Nutrition notes per serving: *288 calories, Protein 9g, Carbohydrate 21g, Fat 19g, Saturated fat 4g, Fibre 3g, Added sugar none, Salt 1.15g.*

MARROW, POTATO AND SAGE SOUP

Until recently, I'd considered marrows a waste of time when it came to soup-making. Well, they don't have a great deal of flavour. I was wrong, as it turns out. Made with a good stock, and fresh herbs, marrow soup can be soothing and most welcome.

Serves 6

1 onion, chopped

1 garlic clove, chopped

40g/1½oz butter

750g/1lb 10oz peeled, diced marrow

350g/12oz diced potato

4 fresh sage leaves

2 tsp sugar

1.2 litres/2 pints vegetable or chicken stock

salt and freshly ground black pepper

150ml/¼ pint single cream

chopped fresh parsley or fresh sage leaves, to garnish

1 In a large pan, cook the onion and garlic gently in the butter until tender, without browning. Add the marrow, potato and sage leaves, coat in the butter, then cover tightly. Sweat over a low heat for 10 minutes, stirring occasionally.

2 Add the sugar, stock, salt and pepper and bring to the boil. Simmer for 20–30 minutes until the vegetables are very tender.

3 Cool slightly, fish out the sage leaves and discard, then liquidize the soup in several batches. Return to the pan, adding extra stock or water, if necessary. Taste and adjust the seasoning.

4 When ready to serve, bring back to the boil, draw off the heat and stir in the single cream. Garnish with chopped parsley or sage leaves.

Nutrition notes per serving: *178 calories, Protein 3g, Carbohydrate 18g, Fat 11g, Saturated fat 7g, Fibre 2g, Added sugar 2g, Salt 0.99g.*

TIP

If you have time, deep-fry a handful of sage leaves for a few seconds, to scatter over the soup just before serving.

Starters

GLOBE ARTICHOKES FILLED WITH LEMON SCRAMBLED EGGS

Globe artichoke cups filled with lemony scrambled eggs make an elegant and substantial starter. Convenient too, as both artichokes and eggs can be prepared several hours in advance.

Serves 4

4 globe artichokes

juice of 1 lemon, plus 2 tbsp

2 tbsp wine vinegar (optional)

6 eggs

finely grated rind ½ lemon

salt and freshly ground black pepper

15g/½oz butter

2 tbsp double cream

1 tbsp chopped fresh dill

1   First get rid of any insects that have made their homes between the leaves by soaking the artichokes, stem up, in a bowl of well-salted water (wedge them together so that they don't bob upright) for 30 minutes or so. Snap off the stem close to the base, pulling away the tougher fibres, and rub the exposed surface with lemon juice to prevent browning.

2   Slice off the top 2.5cm/1in or so of the leaves with a sharp knife. Cook in boiling salted water with the juice of half a lemon or two tablespoons of vinegar, to every 1 litre/2 pints of water for 30–50 minutes depending on size. Again wedge them to keep them upright, but this time with the stem end down. Drain well.

3   When cool enough to handle, gently ease open the leaves, exposing the tight purplish cone of thin leaves in the centre. Twist this out to expose the hairy choke, which can then be scraped away with a teaspoon, leaving a well to be filled with the scrambled egg mixture. Leave to cool completely.

4   Beat the eggs in a bowl with the two tablespoons of lemon juice, the grated rind, salt and pepper. Set the bowl over a pan of simmering water and add the butter and cream. Stir until the eggs are creamy (but not setting into hard lumps). Remove from the heat and stir in the dill. Cool slightly, then spoon into the artichoke cups. Serve cold.

Nutrition notes per serving: *185 calories, Protein 11g, Carbohydrate 2g, Fat 15g, Saturated fat 6g, Fibre trace, Added sugar trace, Salt 0.62g.*

TIP

Eating globe artichokes is one of those delightful rituals of the table which leaves no room for great finesse. Fingers must be employed, at least until you reach the treasure of the base. Prepare thoroughly – lots of napkins, finger bowls if you are making a bid for smartness, and one (or more) large bowls in the centre of the table to take the debris. Now the fun can begin. When eating these cups, start with the inner leaves and gradually work your way outwards. Pull the leaves off, one at a time, scooping up a little of the scrambled egg, then nibble off the nugget of soft artichoke at the leaf base. Finally, tackle the sweet, nutty base by spearing chunks with a fork and mopping up the remaining scrambled egg.

GRILLED SPRING ONIONS AND ASPARAGUS WITH LIME AND COARSE SEA SALT

Grilling spring onions and asparagus gives them a smoky flavour that is enhanced by the spicy sharpness of lime. Serve a mixture of the two, or make it even simpler by using just asparagus or just spring onions. The asparagus should be fairly thin; not sprue but not more than 1cm/½in in diameter.

Serves 1

4 fat spring onions or very thin baby leeks, trimmed

4 asparagus spears, trimmed

olive or sunflower oil

lime wedges and coarse sea salt, to serve

1 Brush the spring onions and asparagus with the oil and grill, turning until patched with brown. Serve immediately with lime wedges and sea salt.

Nutrition notes per serving: *78 calories, Protein 3g, Carbohydrate 3g, Fat 6g, Saturated fat 1g, Fibre 2g, Added sugar none, Salt 1g.*

BAKED ONIONS WITH GOATS' CHEESE

These can be eaten hot or cold. I think they are marginally better hot, but I wouldn't argue the case too vehemently.

Serves 4

4 largish onions, peeled and left whole (See Tip)

115g/4oz young fresh goats' cheese

1 egg

8 pitted black olives, chopped

½ tsp fresh thyme leaves or ¼ tsp dried

2 tbsp chopped fresh parsley

salt and freshly ground black pepper

2 tbsp olive oil

1 Cook the onions in boiling salted water for 15 minutes. Drain and run under the cold tap. Carefully ease out the centre of the onions, leaving a sturdy shell. Sit the onion shells in an oiled ovenproof dish.
2 Preheat the oven to 200C/400F/Gas 6. Chop the onion hearts finely, mix with the goat's cheese and all the remaining ingredients except the oil. Fill the onion shells with this mixture, drizzle over the olive oil and bake for 30 minutes. Eat hot or cold.

Nutrition notes per serving: *213 calories, Protein 8g, Carbohydrate 15g, Fat 14g, Saturated fat 5g, Fibre 3g, Added sugar none, Salt 1.72g.*

TIP

Onions are good keepers in the right conditions. Leave them somewhere cool with good air-circulation and they'll last for months. Check occasionally and throw out any that are developing soft patches. Don't keep onions in the fridge, especially cut onions, even for short periods – unless, of course, you are happy to have onion-flavoured milk and onion-flavoured butter and onion-flavoured anything else that's in there.

FRIED COURGETTE AND MINT SALAD

For this salad, the smaller the courgettes are, the better they will hold their shape.

Serves 4

450g/1lb small courgettes

salt and freshly ground black pepper

3 tbsp extra virgin olive oil

2 garlic cloves, sliced

1½ tbsp red wine vinegar

small bunch of fresh mint leaves, chopped

1 Trim the ends off the courgettes and cut into 5cm/2in lengths. If they are thin, cut pieces in half lengthways. Fatter courgette pieces should be halved, then quartered lengthways. Arrange in a colander, sprinkle with salt and leave for 30 minutes to 1 hour. Rinse and pat dry on kitchen paper.

2 Fry the courgettes briskly in the olive oil with the garlic, until brown and tender adding the garlic when they are almost done. As soon as they are cooked, tip into a shallow dish. Add the wine vinegar and mint and season. Marinate for several hours before serving.

Nutrition notes per serving: *98 calories, Protein 2g, Carbohydrate 3g, Fat 1g, Saturated fat 1g, Fibre 1g, Added sugar trace, Salt 0.25g.*

STUFFED TOMATOES

The stuffing is a classic Sicilian mixture of flavours: currants and pine nuts, here with the sharpness of capers and the saltiness of black olives.

Serves 4

4 medium tomatoes (See Tip)

salt

½ tbsp olive oil

FOR THE STUFFING

1 small red onion, finely chopped

2 garlic cloves, finely chopped

2–3 tbsp olive oil

40g/1½oz stale fine breadcrumbs

25g/1oz pitted black olives, finely chopped

1 tbsp capers, drained and finely chopped

1½ tbsp currants

1 tbsp pine nuts

2 tbsp chopped fresh parsley

salt and freshly ground black pepper

1 Cut the tops off the tomatoes and scoop out the flesh (save the tops and flesh for making sauce). Season the insides with a little salt and leave upside down on a wire rack to drain for 30 minutes or so, while you make the stuffing.

2 Preheat the oven to 200C/400F/Gas 6. Make the stuffing: place the onion, garlic and olive oil in a frying pan and cook over a medium heat until the onion is tender. Add the breadcrumbs, raise the heat slightly and fry until golden (add a little extra oil if necessary). Scoop into a bowl and mix with all the remaining stuffing ingredients.

3 Pack the stuffing into the tomatoes and snuggle them together in an oiled ovenproof dish. Drizzle over the remaining half a tablespoon of olive oil and bake for 15 minutes until nicely browned.

Nutrition notes per serving: *166 calories, Protein 3g, Carbohydrate 15g, Fat 11g, Saturated fat 1g, Fibre 2g, Added sugar trace, Salt 1.04g.*

TIP

Why is it that bought tomatoes are more often than not so disappointing? One reason is that commercially grown tomatoes are picked under-ripe for easy transportation. They ripen off plant, but the flavour never develops its full potential. Luckily, matters have improved lately. Some supermarkets sell tomatoes labelled 'grown for flavour' which can be good. The moral is either grow your own, or be prepared to spend a little more on 'grown for flavour' varieties. For cooking, choose tomatoes that are a deep, ripe red.

Main Courses

SPICED TURNIPS AND CHICK PEAS

This is adapted from a Moroccan recipe for a tangine of lamb, turnips and chick peas. I've jettisoned the lamb but kept the original blend of aromatic spices and the honey sweetener. It is still substantial enough to work as a main course, served over a bed of couscous or rice.

Serves 4

175g/6oz dried chick peas, soaked overnight

675g/1½lb medium turnips, peeled if necessary and cut into 1cm/½in cubes (See Tip)

25g/1oz unsalted butter

1 tbsp sunflower oil

1 onion, coarsely grated

1 tsp ground cinnamon

1 tsp ground ginger

1 tsp ground cumin

½ tbsp ground coriander

1 tbsp clear honey

2 tbsp chopped fresh coriander

salt and freshly ground black pepper

1 Drain the chick peas and cook in unsalted water until almost, but not quite tender. This can take anything from 1½ hours to a staggering 3 hours. Drain, reserving the cooking water. Blanch the turnips for 2 minutes in boiling water, then drain.

2 Melt the butter and oil in a wide pan and add the chick peas, onion, turnips, ground spices and enough of the reserved chick pea water to just cover. Cover and simmer for 15 minutes.

3 Stir in the honey, half the chopped coriander, salt and plenty of pepper. Simmer, uncovered, for 10–15 minutes or until the liquid is reduced to a thick sauce. Sprinkle with the remaining coriander and serve.

Nutrition notes per serving: *278 calories, Protein 12g, Carbohydrate 36g, Fat 11g, Saturated fat 5g, Fibre 8g, Added sugar 4g, Salt 0.36g.*

TIP

In spring, look out for the pretty sight of bunches of glowing quail's egg-sized turnips with their purply pink cheeks and long green leaves. These are turnips at their best. Trim off any leaves (save them) leaving 1cm/½in or so of greenery sticking up for effect and steam the turnips – they won't need peeling. A knob of butter is enough embellishment. The leaves you saved can be eaten, too, as a spinach-like vegetable boiled until tender, drained and fried for a few minutes over a brisk heat in olive oil or butter.

ROOT VEGETABLE PIE ✦

This sturdy root vegetable pie wrapped in puff pastry makes a magnificent main course without breaking the bank. It's one of those recipes that somehow seems to exceed the sum of its parts, tasting ten times better than you might expect.

Serves 4–6

450g/1lb carrots, sliced

450g/1lb potatoes, sliced

225g/8oz turnips, peeled if necessary and sliced

450g/1lb puff pastry, thawed if frozen

2 tbsp finely chopped fresh parsley

2 tsp caraway seeds

salt and freshly ground black pepper

55g/2oz butter, plus extra for greasing

1 egg, beaten

1 Bring a large pan of lightly salted water to the boil. Cook the carrot slices for 6 minutes, then scoop out and drain. Repeat with the potatoes and turnips, keeping each vegetable separate.

2 Butter a loose-bottomed 5cm/2in deep by 20cm/8in diameter cake tin. Roll out two-thirds of the pastry on a lightly floured surface to give a rough circle of about 33cm/13in in diameter. Loosely fold in half, then in quarters, then lift into the tin with the centre tip of the pastry at the centre of the tin. Carefully unfold, then lift the edges and gently push the pastry down to line the sides of the tin using a small knob of pastry rolled into a ball to ease it right into the corners.

3 Make separate layers of potatoes, carrots and turnips, sprinkling parsley, caraway seeds and salt and pepper between the layers and dotting with butter as you go.

4 Roll out the remaining pastry, and lay over the pie. Trim off the excess and press the edges of the pastry together firmly. Make a hole in the centre, then let the pie rest for 30 minutes in the fridge.

5 Preheat the oven to 220C/425F/Gas 7. Brush the top of the pie with beaten egg and bake for 10 minutes until golden brown. Reduce the oven temperature to 180C/350F/Gas 4 and cook for a further 50–60 minutes. Test with a skewer to check that the vegetables are cooked and tender. Unmould carefully and serve hot or warm.

Nutrition notes per serving for four: *683 calories, Protein 12g, Carbohydrate 73g, Fat 40g, Saturated fat 8g, Fibre 6g, Added sugar none, Salt 1.56g.*

✦ *When cold, carefully remove the pie from its tin and wrap in foil. It will keep for up to 1 month. To protect it further, place in a rigid freezer-proof container. Defrost thoroughly, then reheat, covered, until piping hot.*

TIP

As long as you drain the vegetables thoroughly, the pie can be constructed a couple of hours in advance, then whipped into the oven an hour or so before you plan to eat.

PARSNIP, CARROT AND CAULIFLOWER KORMA

This is a mild but warmly spiced curry, thickened with yogurt and ground almonds. Serve with rice, and relishes: mango chutney, sour lime pickles and Indian raw onion chutney (recipe below).

Serves 4

280g/10oz parsnips

350g/12oz carrots

1 medium onion, finely chopped

4 tbsp sunflower oil

1 tbsp ground cumin

2 tsp ground coriander

1 tsp ground cinnamon

1 tsp turmeric

2 garlic cloves, finely chopped

2.5cm/1in piece fresh root ginger, peeled and very finely chopped

1 fresh green chilli, seeded and very finely chopped

300ml/½ pint Greek-style yogurt

45g/1½oz ground almonds

salt

280g/10oz small cauliflower florets

finely chopped fresh coriander or parsley, to garnish

1 Cut the parsnips and carrots into 1cm/½in slices or if they are large, cube them.

2 In a pan large enough to take all the ingredients fry the onion in the oil until golden brown. Stir in all the dry spices and, when well mixed, add the garlic, ginger and chilli. Stir gently for 1 minute. Stir in the yogurt, a tablespoon at a time, then add the almonds. Cook, stirring, for 2 minutes.

3 Stir in 300ml/½ pint of water and some salt, then add the parsnips, carrots and cauliflower. Cover and simmer gently for 20–25 minutes until the vegetables are almost done, stirring occasionally. Uncover the pan and simmer for 5 minutes or so. Taste and adjust the seasoning. Sprinkle with coriander or parsley before serving.

Nutrition notes per serving: *378 calories, Protein 13g, Carbohydrate 25g, Fat 26g, Saturated fat 6g, Fibre 8g, Added sugar none, Salt 0.50g.*

TIP

You can adapt this curry to practically any vegetables that you have to hand, as long as you add those that take less time to cook 5–10 minutes or so after the slow-cooking root vegetables.

INDIAN RAW ONION CHUTNEY

This uncooked 'chutney' takes only a few minutes to make and is a fine accompaniment to any curry. I usually use a red onion which has a sweeter taste than an ordinary white one.

Serves 4

1 large red onion, finely chopped

1 heaped tsp ground cumin

¼–½ tsp chilli powder

½ tsp sweet paprika

2 tbsp fresh lemon juice

1 Mix together all the ingredients. Taste and add a little more cumin or chilli if the chutney needs it.

Nutrition notes per serving: *20 calories, Protein 1g, Carbohydrate 4g, Fat 0.4g, Saturated fat trace, Fibre 1g, Added sugar none, Salt 0.01g.*

THREE-MINUTE FISH WITH CUCUMBER AND CELERY RELISH

The crunchy spiced relish compliments the pure flavour of the briefly cooked fish, but there's no good reason not to serve it with other things. I like it with chicken, too, or even with bread and cheese.

Serves 4–6

550g–675g/1¼–1½lb fillet of salmon or cod, halibut or other firm white fish

olive oil

snipped fresh chives, to garnish

FOR THE RELISH

½ cucumber, finely diced (See Tip)

salt

2 celery stalks, finely diced

4 tbsp rice vinegar or white wine vinegar or tarragon vinegar

1½ tsp peeled and grated fresh root ginger

2 tsp caster sugar

1½ tsp mustard seeds

1 tsp dill seeds

½ medium onion, very finely diced

½–1 green chilli, seeded and very finely chopped

1   Make the relish: spread the diced cucumber out in a colander and sprinkle with half a teaspoon of salt. Leave to drain for 30 minutes, then rinse and pat dry. Mix with the celery.

2   Place the vinegar, ginger, sugar and seeds in a small pan and bring to the boil, stirring to dissolve the sugar. Simmer for 2 minutes, then add the onion and chilli, stir and remove from the heat. Mix with the cucumber and celery. Cool and leave for 30 minutes or up to 24 hours, covered in the fridge.

3   Place the fish in the freezer for 10–15 minutes to firm up. This is not absolutely necessary, but it makes the slicing easier. Slice the fish as thinly as you can. Brush one large or four individual ovenproof dishes with olive oil. Arrange the fish slices in the dish or dishes, overlapping as little as possible. Brush with olive oil.

4   Preheat the oven to its highest setting and when everyone is gathered at the table, whizz the fish into the oven for 3 minutes, or until the slices begin to turn opaque. Scatter over a few chives and serve quickly with the cool relish.

Nutrition notes per serving for four: 169 calories, Protein 26g, Carbohydrate 7g, Fat 4g, Saturated fat 1g, Fibre 1g, Added sugar 3g, Salt 0.57g.

TIP

As long as cucumbers are firm from one tip right through to the other, they are good enough to provide pleasure even if they don't quite measure up to a freshly picked home-grown specimen. Whether I'm using cucumbers raw or cooked, I rarely bother to peel them. I like the look of dark green against pale. Some people find the skins indigestible, and if you're one of them you will peel the skins off whatever I say. Never bother to remove the seeds unless you intend to stuff the cucumbers. It is a totally pointless exercise. I suppose if the cucumber was enormous and the seeds beginning to toughen it might be necessary, but I've never yet come across a bought cucumber that old and past it.

CHICKEN WITH JERUSALEM ARTICHOKE STUFFING

A well-flavoured roast chicken – free-range, not broiler – with a good stuffing makes a first class main course for Sunday lunch. Nuggets of Jerusalem artichoke give this stuffing a most appetizing flavour.

Serves 4

1.5–1.75kg/3–4 lb chicken

15g/½oz butter

salt and freshly ground black pepper

FOR THE STUFFING

450g/1lb Jerusalem artichokes (See Tip)

25g/1oz butter

2 rashers rindless bacon, diced

1 small onion, finely chopped

1 fresh thyme sprig

2 tbsp chopped fresh parsley

85g/3oz soft brown breadcrumbs

3 spring onions, chopped

2 tsp chopped fresh tarragon

½ tsp Worcestershire sauce

1 egg, beaten

1 Make the stuffing: boil the artichokes in their skins until just tender, but not soggy. Cool slightly and peel, then chop finely.

2 Melt the butter in a pan and add the bacon, onion (not the spring onions), thyme and parsley. Cover and sweat for 10 minutes.

3 Remove the lid and raise the heat. Cook, stirring occasionally, until virtually all the liquid has evaporated. Cool slightly. Mix with the artichokes, breadcrumbs, spring onions, tarragon, Worcestershire sauce, salt and pepper, then add enough beaten egg to bind.

4 Preheat the oven to 200C/400F/Gas 6. Fill the chicken with the stuffing. Rub the butter into the skin and season with salt and pepper. Roast, basting occasionally, for 1¼–1½ hours until the chicken juices run clear. Turn off heat. Rest chicken for 10 minutes with the door slightly ajar, before carving.

Nutrition notes per serving: *795 calories, Protein 49g, Carbohydrate 21g, Fat 58g, Saturated fat 20g, Fibre 4g, Added sugar none, Salt 1.78g.*

TIP

If you have the choice, pick out Jerusalem artichokes that are as smooth as possible, which will make them easier to peel. Some people eat the skins, but I find them too tough for my taste. I usually just scrub the artichokes, then steam or boil them in their jackets until tender (or half-cooked depending on the recipe). I leave the peeling until they are done, at which point the skins peel off easily. This is not so practical when you want to serve them straight from the pan, with no more than a knob of butter, in which case you'd better peel them before cooking. Their high iron content makes them prone to greying when exposed to the air, so drop them in acidulated water as you peel, then boil them in acidulated water.

LEEK AND BLACK PUDDING TART ✻

I find large pieces of black pudding too cloying to enjoy, but cut into smaller pieces and mixed with other things, the flavour rather than the texture is what you notice. I love the combination of black pudding and lots of leek in this savoury tart.

Serves 6–8

350g/12oz shortcrust pastry
(page 62)

25g/1oz butter

675g/1½lb leeks, trimmed
and thinly sliced (See Tip)

150ml/¼ pint single cream

2 eggs

2 tbsp finely chopped fresh parsley

2 fresh marjoram sprigs, chopped
or ¼ tsp dried marjoram

55g/2oz Gruyère cheese,
finely grated

salt and freshly ground black pepper

225g/8oz black pudding, skinned and
cut into chunks

1 Line a 25cm/10in tart tin with pastry. Let it rest for 30 minutes in the fridge.

2 Meanwhile, place a baking sheet in the oven, and heat to 200C/400F/Gas 6. Prick the pastry base, then line the tart tin with foil or greaseproof paper and weigh down with baking beans. Place on the hot baking sheet and cook for 10 minutes, remove the beans and paper and return to the oven to dry out for a further 5 minutes. Reduce the oven temperature to 190C/375F/Gas 5.

3 Make the filling: melt the butter in a pan and add the leeks. Cover and cook over a moderate heat for 10–15 minutes until tender, stirring occasionally. Remove from the heat and beat in the cream, then the eggs, parsley, marjoram and half the Gruyère. Season to taste.

4 Scatter the black pudding over the base of the tart and spoon the leek mixture evenly over the top. Sprinkle on the remaining cheese, and bake the tart for 30–35 minutes until just set and golden brown. Serve hot or cold.

Nutrition notes per serving for six: *523 calories, Protein 15g, Carbohydrate 36g, Fat 37g, Saturated fat 18g, Fibre 4g, Added sugar none, Salt 1.89g.*

✻ *Freeze the pie in its tin for up to 1 month. Defrost thoroughly, then reheat, covered, until piping hot.*

TIP

Over-boiled leeks are a disaster – slimy and tasteless, they make grim eating. It's even worse when they've not been properly cleaned in the first place. Earth and grit nestle tightly right down inside the layers of leaves, often further in than you might believe possible. They must be thoroughly cleaned before anything else. To do this, trim off most of the flags (the leaves), then slice from the top down the centre of the leek roughly to the middle, or even a little further. A second cut, at right angles to the first, makes them easier to clean, but if you want large pieces you'll have to manage without. Wash the leeks, under the cold tap, splaying them out where you've cut them and making sure you rinse off every last bit of grit. The coarse green flags need not be wasted – use them for making soup, or throw them into the stockpot.

ROAST POUSSINS WITH FENNEL

Fennel provides the essential boost that mild-flavoured poussins need if they are to be at all interesting. It is used to flavour not only the birds as they roast but also the sauce that will be served with them.

Serves 2 generously

1 large fennel bulb (See Tip)

2 poussins

45g/1½oz butter

salt and freshly ground black pepper

1 tbsp plain flour

250ml/9fl oz milk

90ml/3fl oz single cream

freshly grated nutmeg

1 Preheat the oven to 200C/400F/Gas 6. Trim a thin slice off the base of the fennel and discard the stalks, which tend to be stringy. If the outer layer of the fennel is looking ropey remove that as well. Reserve the green leaves, and quarter the bulb from top to base. Place one quarter inside each poussin, then finely dice the remaining two quarters.

2 Smear the breasts of the poussins with half the butter, and season with salt and pepper. Sit the poussins in a roasting tin and roast for 30–40 minutes until cooked through.

3 While they cook, melt the remaining butter and add the diced fennel (but not the fronds). Stir, then cover and sweat over a low heat for 15 minutes. Remove the lid and sprinkle in the flour. Cook for 1 minute, stirring.

4 Gradually add the milk a little at a time, stirring well, to make a smooth sauce. Add the cream, bring to the boil and simmer gently for 5–8 minutes, stirring occasionally. Season with salt, pepper and nutmeg to taste. If not serving immediately, spear a small knob of butter on a fork and rub over the surface of the sauce to prevent a skin forming.

5 Just before serving, reheat the sauce, adding a little extra milk if it seems over-thick when warm. Stir in the fennel fronds and serve with the poussins.

Nutrition notes per serving: *1036 calories, Protein 59g, Carbohydrate 19g, Fat 81g, Saturated fat 34g, Fibre 5g, Added sugar none, Salt 1.67g.*

TIP

Fennel is a marvellous vegetable with a unique aniseed taste. Or at least I think it is a marvellous vegetable, but I can understand why some people may dislike it. It announces its presence in no uncertain way, particularly when eaten raw. That's what I like about it. No namby-pamby background recluse, Fennel tastes strong and refreshing in a salad. Heat, though, induces a remarkable change, tempering the assertive flavour down to a mellow but distinctive sweetness. The vegetable (properly known as Florence fennel) is obviously closely related to the fennel herb, but the plants are not identical. Florence fennel is grown for its tightly packed 'heads' or 'bulbs' which are actually swollen basal stems of the plant. Having said that, its feathery leaves can also be used as a herb.

POTATO AND PEPPER STEW

This makes a perfect supper dish, as long as you get good *chorizo* to enliven the mixture. Serve with plenty of good bread to mop up the juices.

Serves 4

3 tbsp olive oil

115g/4oz cooking *chorizo*, skinned and roughly sliced (See Tip)

1.25kg/2lb 12oz potatoes, cut into roughly 2.5cm/1in chunks

1 red and 1 green pepper, seeded and diced

2 garlic cloves, crushed

½ tbsp Spanish paprika (*pimentón*)

1 bay leaf

salt and freshly ground black pepper

1 Warm the oil over a moderate heat in an earthernware *cazuela* or a wide heavy frying pan. Add the *chorizo* and fry briskly until lightly browned. It will fall to pieces, but this doesn't matter.

2 Reduce the heat and add all the remaining ingredients. Pour over just enough water to cover. Bring to the boil and simmer, stirring occasionally, for 20–30 minutes, until the potatoes are cooked and the liquid has reduced by about half. Taste and adjust the seasoning, then serve.

Nutrition notes per serving: *428 calories, Protein 13g, Carbohydrate 58g, Fat 17g, Saturated fat 4g, Fibre 5g, Added sugar none, Salt 1.26g.*

TIP

Spanish *chorizo* is a delicious type of cured pork sausage flavoured with paprika. It can be either mild (*dulce*) or hot and spicy (*picante*). There's another choice to be made, too. Some *chorizo* is dried fairly hard, like a salami, ideal served thinly sliced as part of an hors d'oeuvre. What you want for cooking is the softer sort, semi-dried, usually not more than 2.5cm/1in in diameter. This is what I mean by cooking *chorizo*. Don't be tempted to buy what is sometimes described as 'Spanish-style *chorizo*'. It's disgusting.

TUNA WITH SWEET-AND-SOUR ONIONS

I first ate this in a small restaurant just off one of Palermo's main streets during a trip to Sicily. The sharp sweet onions set off the richness of tuna perfectly.

Serves 4

4 x 7–8 oz tuna steaks about 2cm/¾in thick

salt and freshly ground black pepper

4 tbsp olive oil

2 large red onions, thinly sliced

1 level tbsp caster sugar

3 tbsp red wine vinegar

90ml/3fl oz dry white wine

2 tbsp chopped fresh parsley

1 Season the tuna steaks with salt and pepper.

2 Warm three tablespoons of the olive oil in a wide frying pan and add the onions. Cook gently until soft, then raise the heat to medium and fry the onions until richly browned. Scoop out and reserve.

3 Add the remaining oil to the pan and heat thoroughly. Fry the tuna steaks briskly on both sides to brown. Reduce the heat and cook for 1 minute. Now add the sugar, vinegar and wine, then return the onions to the pan and stir around the tuna. Turn up the heat to high, cover and simmer for 2 minutes. Sprinkle with parsley and serve.

Nutrition notes per serving: *316 calories, Protein 38g, Carbohydrate 9g, Fat 13g, Saturated fat 2g, Fibre 1g, Added sugar 3g, Salt 0.42g.*

PRAWN AND BROAD BEAN PILAU

This is an incredibly delicious pilau, packed with broad beans and shrimps and delicately spiced. It is best, naturally, made with fresh broad beans, though it is not bad made with frozen ones either. To make it really special, blanch and skin the beans (See Tip) before adding them to the rice.

Serves 4

1 large onion, chopped

2 garlic cloves, chopped

2 tbsp sunflower oil

1 tsp turmeric

1 tsp cumin seeds, bruised with a pestle or the end of a rolling pin

1 tsp fennel seeds, bruised

225g/8oz basmati or other long grain rice, rinsed

salt and freshly ground black pepper

280–450g/10oz–1lb shelled broad beans, thawed if frozen

225g/8oz shelled cooked prawns

2 tbsp chopped fresh coriander

FOR THE RAITA

¼ cucumber

salt

300ml/½ pint Greek-style yogurt

1 Make the raita: grate the cucumber coarsely without peeling it. Spread it out in a colander and sprinkle with salt. Leave for 30 minutes to 1 hour. Squeeze out excess moisture, then dry on kitchen paper. Mix into the yogurt and set aside.

2 In a large pan, cook the onion and garlic gently in the oil for a couple of minutes. Add the spices and continue cooking until the onion is tender. Stir in the rice and cook for a further 1 minute.

3 Add 600ml/1 pint of water, salt and pepper and bring to the boil. If you are using fresh whole broad beans add these now. Reduce to a simmer, cover tightly and leave to cook for 10 minutes.

4 Add the prawns and thawed frozen broad beans, if using. Stir, then cover again and cook for 5–10 minutes until the rice is tender and all the liquid has been absorbed. If necessary, add a little more hot water as the pilau cooks. Stir in the coriander, then taste and adjust the seasoning. Serve with the cool raita.

Nutrition notes per serving: *458 calories, Protein 27g, Carbohydrate 57g, Fat 15g, Saturated fat 5g, Fibre 5g, Added sugar none, Salt 2.92g.*

TIP

I'm well aware of the fact that many people loathe broad beans. It's the tough grey outer skin that is the culprit, imparting a coarse flavour and texture and getting irritatingly stuck between the teeth. Take time to remove the skin and broad beans are transformed into a completely new vegetable, like a butterfly emerging from a chrysalis. The inner beanlets have a brilliant green colour, a vivid flavour and a marvellous mealy softness. To skin fresh, shelled broad beans, drop them into a pan of boiling water and blanch for 1 minute. Drain, run under the cold tap, then slit the skin of each bean and squeeze out the beanlet. To skin frozen broad beans (broad beans freeze very well), either let them thaw, or place in a bowl and cover with boiling water, leaving for a minute or so before draining. Then the skins will slip off easily.

ASPARAGUS AND GRUYÈRE QUICHE ❄

This is a quiche to make at the height of the asparagus season when you've feasted your fill of plainly cooked asparagus. It is an excellent way of stretching a small quantity of asparagus.

Serves 6–8

350g/12oz shortcrust pastry (page 62)

350g/12oz asparagus (See Tip)

115g/4oz Gruyère cheese

3 shallots or 1 small onion, chopped

15g/½oz butter

3 eggs

150ml/¼ pint milk

90ml/3fl oz double cream

1 tbsp chopped fresh chervil or fresh parsley

salt and freshly ground black pepper

1 Line a 23cm/9in tart tin with the pastry. Leave it to rest in the fridge for 30 minutes. Preheat the oven to 200C/400F/Gas 6.

2 Prick the base of the tart with a fork and line with greaseproof paper or foil and weigh down with baking beans. Bake for 10 minutes. Remove paper or foil and beans and return to the oven for 5 minutes to dry out. Leave to cool. Reduce the oven temperature to 180C/350F/Gas 4.

3 Trim the asparagus, breaking off the tough ends (save these and their cooking water for making soup). Cut into 2cm/¾in lengths, keeping the tips separate.

4 Pour 4cm/1½in of water into a large pan, add salt and bring to the boil. Add the stem pieces of asparagus and simmer for 5 minutes. Add the tips and simmer gently for 2–3 minutes, until almost *al dente*, but still firm. Drain. If prepared in advance, cool and cover.

5 Dice 85g/3oz of the Gruyère and grate the remaining cheese. Fry the shallots or onion gently in the butter until tender, without browning. Scatter the asparagus, diced Gruyère and shallots over the base of the pastry case.

6 Whisk the eggs lightly, then whisk in the milk, cream, chervil or parsley and salt and pepper. Pour over the asparagus and cheese. Scatter grated Gruyère over the top and bake for 25–30 minutes, until just set in the centre and nicely browned. Serve hot, warm or cold.

Nutrition notes per serving for six: *487 calories, Protein 14g, Carbohydrate 29g, Fat 36g, Saturated fat 19g, Fibre 2g, Added sugar none, Salt 0.92g.*

❄ *Freeze the pie in its tin for up to 1 month. Defrost thoroughly, then reheat, covered, until piping hot.*

TIP

Green-stemmed asparagus, the type we grow in Britain, is graded into three sizes. The fashionable sprue is the spindly, extremely tender type which requires only a few minutes cooking. Growers, however, consider sprue the poor relation – not much to sink your teeth into. 'Best' is medium-thick, around 1cm/½in in diameter. Then there are the 'Specials': big, fat and juicy, the prime asparagus fit for a king.

Side Dishes

RATATOUILLE

There is no point trying to make ratatouille in a smaller quantity than this. And why should you? It keeps well in the fridge for a couple of days, and tastes even better cold than hot.

Serves 6–8

1 large aubergine, cut into 2.5cm/1in chunks

450g/1lb courgettes, cut into 1cm/½in thick slices

½ tbsp salt

1 large onion, chopped

2 garlic cloves, chopped

4 tbsp olive oil

1 green and 1 red pepper, halved, seeded and cut into 1cm/½in wide strips

400g can chopped tomatoes or 450g/1lb fresh tomatoes, skinned and roughly chopped

1 tbsp tomato purée

½ tsp sugar

salt and freshly ground black pepper

½ tbsp coriander seeds, crushed

2 tbsp chopped fresh basil or fresh parsley, to garnish

extra virgin olive oil (optional)

1 Place the aubergine and courgettes in separate colanders and sprinkle with the salt. Leave for 30 minutes to drain. Rinse then pat dry on kitchen paper.

2 In a wide frying pan, or pan, cook the onion and garlic gently in the oil until tender, without browning. Add the aubergine and peppers, stir, then cover and cook for 10 minutes, stirring once or twice.

3 Now add the courgettes, tomatoes, tomato purée, sugar, salt and pepper. Bring to the boil, then lower the heat and simmer gently, uncovered, for about 30 minutes, stirring occasionally to prevent burning.

4 Stir in the coriander seeds and continue cooking until all trace of wateriness has gone and the ratatouille is thick and rich. Taste and adjust the seasonings, adding a little sugar if it is on the sharp side. Serve hot or cold sprinkled with basil or parsley and maybe a drizzle of extra virgin olive oil.

Nutrition notes per serving for six: *137 calories, Protein 4g, Carbohydrate 12g, Fat 8g, Saturated fat 1g, Fibre 5g, Added sugar 0.4g, Salt 0.59g.*

TIP

Like the little girl with the curl, when it's good, ratatouille is very, very good, but when it's bad, it's horrid. There are different theories about how to make the perfect ratatouille. Some people insist on cooking all the vegetables separately, combining them only for the last few minutes. True, they keep their individual shapes better that way, but I prefer the more standard approach. I always cook them together, adding them in stages, so that the flavours all intermingle. The key to making a good ratatouille is, in my opinion, slow, lazy burbling on top of the stove (the stew that is, not you or me). Never rush the cooking process. Allow plenty of time for the dish to mellow to a Provençal richness.

BROCCOLI WITH CHILLI AND PARMESAN

This is a quick way to dress up cooked broccoli with a dash of fire.

Serves 4

675g/1½lb broccoli

salt

3 tbsp olive oil

¼–½ tsp chilli flakes

2–3 garlic cloves, finely chopped

15g/½oz Parmesan cheese, cut into paper-thin slivers

1   Separate the broccoli florets from the stalks. Slice the stalks about 1cm/½in thick, then drop the stalks into a pan of lightly salted boiling water. Simmer for 2 minutes, then add the florets and cook for a further 2–3 minutes until almost but not quite done. Drain, run under the cold tap to refresh, then leave to drain completely and pat dry with kitchen paper.

2   Heat the oil in a wide frying pan, and add the chilli flakes and garlic. Cook over a low heat for 1 minute, then add the broccoli. Raise the heat a little and stir fry for 4–5 minutes until the broccoli is piping hot. Tip into a serving dish and scatter over the Parmesan.

Nutrition notes per serving: *151 calories, Protein 9g, Carbohydrate 4g, Fat 11g, Saturated fat 2g, Fibre 5g, Added sugar none, Salt 0.39g.*

TIP

It is a mistake to steam broccoli. It tastes fine, but it turns a grim murky green that is far from attractive. Instead, I either boil or microwave it so that it retains its bright colour. I've been shocked to hear that some people throw away large parts of the stalk. It's the best bit.

SULTAN'S DELIGHT

Aubergines are terrifically important in Turkish cuisine and used for all sorts of dishes. This is delicious served with grilled meats or stews.

Serves 4

2 large aubergines weighing about 675g/1½lb in total

40g/1½oz butter

40g/1½oz plain flour

425ml/¾ pint milk

55g/2oz Parmesan, freshly grated

salt and freshly ground black pepper

chopped fresh parsley, to garnish

1   Grill the aubergines whole, turning frequently, until blackened and blistered all over and soft to the touch. Drop into a plastic bag and leave until cool enough to handle. Cut in half, skin, then chop the flesh roughly. Pile into a colander and drain for 30 minutes. Press to squeeze out the bitter juices.

2   Melt the butter and stir in the flour. Stir for a few minutes until biscuit-coloured. Off the heat, beat in the milk a little at a time to form a white sauce. Bring back to the boil and simmer for 10 minutes until thick.

3   Place the aubergines and sauce in a food processor and blend together. If you don't have a processor, chop the aubergines finely, then mash as thoroughly as you can before mixing into the sauce. Return to the heat, stir in the Parmesan, season to taste and warm through, stirring. Spoon on to a warm serving dish and scatter with parsley.

Nutrition notes per serving: *266 calories, Protein 11g, Carbohydrate 17g, Fat 18g, Saturated fat 11g, Fibre 4g, Added sugar none, Salt 0.98g.*

FRENCH BEANS WITH CUMIN AND ALMONDS

Who would have thought that adding a spoonful of cumin and a few almonds to a panful of French beans would turn them into something so exotic? Well, it does, though they are not so over-the-top exotic as to clash with an otherwise straightforward meal.

Serves 4

2 tbsp olive or sunflower oil or 25g/1oz butter

15g/½oz flaked almonds

1 small onion, chopped

450g/1lb French beans, topped and tailed and cut into 2.5–4cm/1–1½in lengths (See Tip)

1 tsp ground cumin

salt and freshly ground black pepper

1   Heat the oil or butter in a wide frying pan and fry the almonds briskly until golden brown. Scoop out and drain on kitchen paper.

2   Reduce the heat under the pan and fry the onion until tender without browning. Add the beans, cumin and salt and pepper and fry for 3 minutes.

3   Add two tablespoons of water, then cover and cook for 5 minutes or until the beans are tender and most of the liquid has been absorbed. Return the almonds to the pan, stir for a few seconds to reheat, then serve.

Nutrition notes per serving: *109 calories, Protein 3g, Carbohydrate 6g, Fat 8g, Saturated fat 1g, Fibre 3g, Added sugar none, Salt 0.25g.*

TIP

Always choose beans that are crisp and firm – floppy limpness is an unmistakeable 'steer-clear' signal. To prepare, just top and tail, pulling off any strings as you work (unless they are very small in which case don't bother).

CREAMED LEEKS WITH ORANGE

This cross between a vegetable side dish and a sauce was something I originally came up with to serve with roast pork, and very good partners they were too. However, the creamed leeks are so delicious that I've since served them with fish, fowl and vegetable.

Serves 4–6

40g/1½oz butter

5 large leeks, trimmed, cut into 4–5cm/1½–2in lengths and finely shredded

juice and finely grated rind of 1 orange

salt and freshly ground black pepper

40g/1½oz plain flour

300ml/½ pints milk

squeeze of fresh lemon juice

1   Melt the butter in a wide pan and add the leeks. Stir to mix, then add the orange juice and a little seasoning. Cover and simmer for 10 minutes or so, stirring occasionally, until the leeks are just tender. Uncover and boil off most of the watery juices until just a few tablespoons of buttery liquid remain.

2   Sprinkle over the flour and stir to mix evenly. Gradually add the milk, stirring, then the grated orange rind. Bring to a simmer and cook for 3–5 minutes until very thick and creamy. If absolutely necessary add a little more milk. Season and stir in the lemon juice. Taste and adjust the seasoning. If not using immediately, spear a small knob of butter on the tip of a knife and rub over the surface to prevent a skin forming.

Nutrition notes per serving for four: *189 calories, Protein 5g, Carbohydrate 16g, Fat 12g, Saturated fat 7g, Fibre 3g, Added sugar none, Salt 0.55g.*

BAKED NEW POTATOES WITH ANCHOVY AND PARSLEY

There's no law to say that new potatoes should only be boiled or steamed. Baking them slowly in the oven gives them a luxurious buttery texture.

Serves 4–6

900g/2lb new potatoes

45g/1½oz butter

3 tbsp olive oil

3 anchovy fillets, drained and chopped (See Tip)

2 garlic cloves, crushed with a little salt

2 tbsp chopped fresh parsley

2 tbsp fresh lemon juice

salt and freshly ground black pepper

1   Preheat the oven to 200C/400F/Gas 6. Scrub the potatoes, removing as much skin as you can. Halve or quarter larger ones. Pat dry on kitchen paper.

2   In a flameproof roasting tin, heat the butter with the oil, add the anchovy fillets and cook for 1 minute or so, mashing the fillets into the oil with a fork. Add the potatoes and fry for 4 minutes or until they are beginning to colour. Stir in the garlic and parsley and pour in 150ml/¼ pint of water at arm's length (it's bound to spit back at you). Add the lemon juice, a little salt and plenty of pepper.

3   Transfer the tin to the oven and bake the potatoes for 25–30 minutes, stirring and basting every 10 minutes or so, until browned and meltingly tender. Spoon the potatoes into a warm dish and pour over the pan juices.

Nutrition notes per serving for four: *317 calories, Protein 5g, Carbohydrate 37g, Fat 18g, Saturated fat 6g, Fibre 3g, Added sugar none, Salt 0.75g.*

TIP

The anchovy fillets dissolve into the pan juices without giving an overly fishy flavour, so the potatoes are good with any main course, fish, meat or vegetable.

BEETROOT PURÉE

This is so pretty. Beetroot makes the most beautiful deep pink purée that tastes every bit as good as it looks. I first made it to go with roast pheasant, but it would sit happily alongside any main course that can take its rich earthy taste.

Serves 4

225–280g/8–10oz cooked, peeled beetroot, roughly chopped

225g/8oz floury potatoes, cooked and roughly chopped

90ml/3fl oz soured cream

1 tbsp chopped fresh dill or 1 tsp dried

salt and freshly ground black pepper

25g/1oz butter

1   Place the beetroot and potatoes together with the soured cream, dill, salt and pepper in a food processor and whizz until smooth. Taste and adjust the seasoning.

2   Reheat gently with the butter when needed.

Nutrition notes per serving: *158 calories, Protein 3g, Carbohydrate 16g, Fat 10g, Saturated fat 6g, Fibre 2g, Added sugar none, Salt 0.56g.*

Salads

MOROCCAN SALAD

Cumin is the spice that I associate most strongly with Morocco. It goes into all manner of dishes, hot and cold, lending its warm aromatic scent.

Serves 4–6

2 large green peppers, quartered and seeded

450g/1lb ripe tomatoes, skinned, seeded and chopped (See Tip)

FOR THE DRESSING

1 tbsp fresh lemon juice

3 tbsp extra virgin olive oil

1 large garlic clove, crushed

½ tsp ground cumin

2 tbsp finely chopped fresh parsley or a mixture of parsley and fresh coriander

salt and freshly ground black pepper

1. Grill the peppers, skin sides to the heat, until blackened and blistered. Drop into a plastic bag, knot the ends and leave until cool enough to handle. Strip off the skins, then cut into small pieces. Mix with the tomatoes and any juice given out by the peppers.
2. Mix together the dressing ingredients and toss with the tomatoes and peppers. Serve at room temperature.

Nutrition notes per serving for four: *110 calories, Protein 2g, Carbohydrate 6g, Fat 9g, Saturated fat 1g, Fibre 3g, Added sugar none, Salt 0.29g.*

TIP

To skin tomatoes: simply cover with boiling water, leave for a couple of minutes, then drain, The skin should pull away easily. If it still clings stubbornly, repeat the process. To seed the tomatoes: either cut in half horizontally and scoop out the seeds with a teaspoon or just squeeze the seeds out.

CARROT AND MINT SALAD

If you grow your own carrots, use the slender thinnings to make this salad of fried carrots with mint. If you are not so lucky, then look out for tiny baby carrots, 4cm/1½in or so long. Failing that, get the smallest carrots you can and cut them into suitably sized pieces. As the carrots fry slowly in the olive oil, they caramelize on the outside to an intense earthy sweetness. Dressed with lemon juice and mint, they make an excellent hors d'oeuvre.

Serves 4

450g/1lb baby carrots or small carrots

3 tbsp olive oil

juice of ½ lemon

2 tbsp chopped fresh mint

salt and freshly ground black pepper

1. If you are using baby carrots, just trim off the tops and any tails. If using small carrots, top and tail, then quarter lengthways and cut each piece in half.
2. Heat the oil in a wide, heavy frying pan and add the carrots. Fry slowly, shaking and turning now and then, until the carrots are patched with brown and tender. This takes about 20 minutes. Tip into a bowl and mix with the lemon juice, mint, salt and pepper. Cool and serve at room temperature.

Nutrition notes per serving: *110 calories, Protein 1g, Carbohydrate 7g, Fat 9g, Saturated fat 1g, Fibre 3g, Added sugar none, Salt 0.36g.*

CHICORY AND WALNUT SALAD

Chicory and walnuts are perfect bedfellows, making the best of autumn or winter salads.

Serves 4

3 large heads of chicory

55g/2oz walnut pieces

FOR THE DRESSING

½ tbsp white wine vinegar

¼ tsp Dijon mustard

salt and freshly ground black pepper

2½–3 tbsp groundnut or sunflower oil

1   Make the dressing in the salad bowl: whisk the vinegar with the mustard, salt and pepper, then gradually beat in the oil, a tablespoon at a time. Taste and adjust the seasoning. Cross your salad servers in the bowl.

2   Cut the bases off the chicory heads and discard along with any damaged outer leaves. Separate the heads into individual leaves and pile on top of the salad servers in the bowl. Scatter with the walnuts and toss just before eating.

Nutrition notes per serving: *169 calories, Protein 3g, Carbohydrate 3g, Fat 16g, Saturated fat 2g, Fibre 1g, Added sugar none, Salt 0.27g.*

ANNABEL'S CAULIFLOWER SALAD

Annabel assists me in the kitchen, testing recipes, adjusting them so that they work, and often passing on her own good ideas. This salad is a favourite of hers, and rightly so. It's a lovely combination of flavours and textures, with that extra lift given by the horseradish.

Serves 4–6

15g/½oz flaked almonds

1 cauliflower head, broken into florets

8 tbsp soured cream

1 tbsp creamed horseradish

squeeze of fresh lemon juice

salt and freshly ground black pepper

2 tbsp snipped fresh chives

1   Preheat the oven to 200C/400F/Gas 6. Spread the almonds out on a baking sheet and place in the oven for 3–7 minutes, shaking occasionally, until golden brown. Cool.

2   Drop the cauliflower florets into a pan of lightly salted water and simmer until barely *al dente* – just tender but with a slight crunch to them. Drain and run under the cold tap to prevent further cooking. Drain thoroughly and pat dry.

3   Mix together the soured cream, horseradish, lemon juice and seasoning. Taste and adjust the seasoning. Set aside a few almonds and chives to use as a garnish, then toss the remaining almonds, chives and cauliflower in the soured cream dressing. Scatter with the reserved almonds and chives and serve at room temperature.

Nutrition notes per serving for four: *163 calories, Protein 8g, Carbohydrate 7g, Fat 12g, Saturated fat 5g, Fibre 3g, Added sugar none, Salt 0.41g.*

TIP

Whenever possible, buy cauliflowers that are still surrounded by a ruff of green leaves. The leaves are a better indication of freshness than the look of the white centre itself. If they are limp the cauliflower has been away from the earth for far too long. The curd itself should be firm and creamy with a pleasant smell. Slight discolouration here and there is nothing to worry about.

SALADE CAUCHOISE

This salad from the Pays de Caux in Northern France sets the crispness of celery against the softness of potatoes, with strips of ham in a creamy dressing.

Serves 6

675g/1½lb waxy salad potatoes or new potatoes, scrubbed

6 celery stalks, sliced

115g/4oz cooked ham, cut into strips

fresh chervil or fresh parsley sprigs

FOR THE DRESSING

4 tsp cider vinegar

1½ tbsp chopped fresh chervil or fresh parsley

1½ tbsp snipped fresh chives

salt and freshly ground black pepper

8 tbsp crème fraîche (See Tip)

1 Make the dressing: stir the vinegar, herbs, salt and pepper into the crème fraîche. Taste and adjust the seasoning.

2 Steam the potatoes until tender. While still warm, cut into cubes and toss in half of the dressing. Leave to cool. I think it is a waste of time to try to remove odd pieces of skin, but if you are feeling pernickety strip them off before cutting up the cooked potatoes.

3 Mix the celery and ham with the potatoes with enough extra dressing to coat without overwhelming. Arrange chervil or parsley sprigs on top.

Nutrition notes per serving: *188 calories, Protein 7g, Carbohydrate 20g, Fat 10g, Saturated fat 5g, Fibre 2g, Added sugar trace, Salt 0.91g.*

TIP

I sometimes replace the crème fraîche with fromage frais – not authentic, but still French and still good.

GRILLED AUBERGINE SALAD

A favourite salad of mine – a dark gleaming mass of aubergines, smoky and rich with a garlicky hiss. Grilled aubergine slices, simply salted, then brushed with oil and seasoned before grilling, are good hot too.

Serves 6

2 large aubergines, cut into 1cm/½in thick discs

salt

2–3 tbsp chopped mixed fresh herbs – parsley, basil and/or chives

FOR THE DRESSING

1½ tbsp white or red wine vinegar

1–2 garlic cloves, crushed

salt and freshly ground black pepper

7 tbsp extra virgin olive oil

1 Make the dressing: mix together the vinegar, garlic, pepper and a little salt, then whisk in the olive oil a tablespoon at a time.

2 Sprinkle the aubergines with salt and leave for 30 minutes to 1 hour. Wipe dry and toss with half the dressing. Preheat the grill to hot. Grill the aubergine slices close to the heat, until browned on both sides. Toss with enough of the remaining dressing to moisten, then leave to cool. Toss with the herbs and serve.

Nutrition notes per serving: *152 calories, Protein 2g, Carbohydrate 5g, Fat 14g, Saturated fat 2g, Fibre 5g, Added sugar trace, Salt 0.35g.*

Chutneys & Preserves

ODED SCHWARTZ'S CARROT AND ALMOND CHUTNEY

When master-pickler Oded Schwartz sent a jar of this irresistible chutney into the production office we simply couldn't stop eating it. The jar was passed around and around, with everyone dipping in, until it was all gone. Chutney or *chatni*, as it is known in Hindi, originated in India but Oded's chutney is derived from various recipes, including Carrot Halwa, an Indian sweet, and a similar Jewish confection served at Passover. Oded recommends serving it with lamb, or hard, mature cheese. I like it so much I'm perfectly happy to eat it neat.

Makes about 2.25kg/5lb

900g/2lb carrots

150g/5oz peeled fresh root ginger

finely grated rind and juice
of 2 lemons

pinch of ground chilli or to taste

25g/1oz salt

25g/1oz ground coriander

500ml/18fl oz cider vinegar

125ml/4fl oz clear honey

675g/1½lb sugar

60g/2¼oz flaked almonds

1 Grate the carrots coarsely lengthways to achieve the longest possible strands. Cut half the ginger into matchsticks and grate the remainder finely. Mix the carrots and all the ginger with the lemon rind and juice, chilli, salt and coriander. Cover with the vinegar and leave overnight.

2 Transfer the marinated carrots and their juices to a preserving pan and add 300ml/½ pint of water. Bring to the boil and simmer for 20 minutes. Add the honey and sugar and stir to dissolve.

3 Bring back to the boil and boil for 25 minutes or until the mixture is thick. Stir in the almonds and boil for a further 4–5 minutes. Spoon into hot sterilized jars (See Tip) and seal immediately. The chutney can be eaten straightaway, although it will improve after storing for a few months.

Nutrition notes per 25g/1oz: *48 calories, Protein 0.3g, Carbohydrate 11g, Fat 0.5g, Saturated fat trace, Fibre 0.3g, Added sugar 10g, Salt 0.32g.*

TIP

To sterilize jars: wash in warm soapy water, then rinse in hot water. Without touching the insides, set upside-down on a wire rack in the oven set to 110C/225F/Gas ½. Leave for at least 30 minutes.

AUBERGINES PRESERVED IN OLIVE OIL

Serve as part of an antipasto with salami, cured ham, olives, cheese and plenty of crusty bread.

Serves 6–8

450g/1lb aubergine

salt

150ml/¼ pint white wine vinegar

150–200ml/¼ pint–7fl oz extra virgin oil

150–200ml/1/4 pint–7fl oz sunflower oil

4 garlic cloves, finely chopped

1–3 fresh red chillies, finely chopped

leaves of 2 fresh thyme sprigs or ½ tsp dried thyme

1   Slice the aubergine into 2.5cm/1in thick discs, then into 2.5cm/1in wide strips. Layer in a large colander, sprinkling each layer with salt. Set aside for 4 hours, turning occasionally, then rinse under cold water.

2   Place the strips in a pan with the vinegar and just enough water to cover. Bring to the boil and simmer for 5–10 minutes until tender. Drain and pat dry.

3   Mix 150ml/¼ pint olive oil with an equal quantity of sunflower oil. Mix the garlic, chilli and thyme together. Pour enough oil to cover the base of a sterilized preserving jar (See Tip page 54), then sprinkle with a little of the garlic, chilli and thyme mixture. Add a layer of aubergines, sprinkle with the garlic mixture, then cover with oil. Repeat, covering the final layer generously with oil.

4   Cover loosely and stand in a cool place for 1–2 hours to settle. If necessary, add more oil to cover completely. Seal tightly and keep in a cool, dry, dark place for at least a week and up to 6 months.

Nutrition notes per serving for six: *91 calories, Protein 1g, Carbohydrate 2g, Fat 9g, Saturated fat 1g, Fibre 2g, Added sugar trace, Salt 0.18g.*

BREAD AND BUTTER PICKLES ⓕ

I adore these pickles, but I've often wondered how they got their name. I don't know for sure, but I suspect it is merely because they are good enough to eat neat with nothing more than thickly buttered bread. Mind you, a slice of mature cheese goes down well alongside.

Fills 2–3 450g/1lb jars

1 large cucumber, peeled and sliced into 3mm/⅛in thick discs

1 red or white onion, very thinly sliced

1 green pepper, seeded and cut into strips

1½ tbsp coarse sea salt

300ml/½ pint white wine vinegar

280g/10oz caster sugar

1 tbsp mustard seeds

1 tsp celery seeds or dill seeds

5cm/2in cinnamon stick

6 allspice berries

pinch of cayenne pepper

1   Mix the cucumber with the onion, green pepper and salt in a bowl. Sit a plate or saucer on top, weigh down with a tin or weights and leave in the fridge for 4–12 hours or overnight. Drain and rinse under cold running water. Taste the cucumber and if it seems too salty rinse again, then drain thoroughly.

2   Place the remaining ingredients in a large pan and stir over a medium heat until the sugar has dissolved. Simmer for 1 minute. Add the vegetables, stir once and bring to a bare simmer without boiling. Spoon into hot sterilized jars (See Tip page 54) and seal tightly. Store in a cool, dark, dry place for up to 4 months.

Nutrition notes per tablespoon: *21 calories, Protein 0.2g, Carbohydrate 5g, Fat trace, Saturated fat trace, Fibre trace, Added sugar 5g, Salt 0.07g.*

TIP

These pickles can be eaten after three or four days, but they will taste even better after three weeks.

Puddings

TURKISH CANDIED SQUASH Ⓕ

A friend of the family gave a recipe for this Turkish pudding to my mother many years ago. It quickly became a family favourite. Since then, I've come across it in Turkish cookery books with slight variations, but always the same basic intent. It is the best pumpkin or squash pudding I have ever come across, but it is very sweet indeed, so serve in small portions. A fairly densely fleshed squash, such as butternut or Red Kuri is easiest to handle. Straight pumpkin is softer and has a tendency to collapse, but as long as you don't mind the pudding looking a little mushier than it should, pumpkin does a fine job.

Serves 4–6

1kg/2¼lb wedge of winter squash such as Red Kuri or butternut or pumpkin (See Tip)

225g/8oz caster sugar

crème fraîche, whipped cream or Greek-style yogurt and 115g/4oz walnuts, roughly chopped, to serve

1   Trim off the rind and discard squash seeds, then cut into 2.5cm/1in chunks. Layer with the sugar in a wide pan and pour over 125ml/4fl oz of water.

2   Cover tightly and cook over a very low heat for about 1 hour, turning the pumpkin carefully occasionally. Towards the end of the cooking time have a look in the pan to assess the liquid level. If it is copious, uncover and let the liquid boil down to a thick syrup. Cool in the pan.

3   Spoon into individual dishes and chill. Top with a dollop of crème fraîche, cream or yogurt, then scatter with walnuts.

Nutrition notes per serving for four: *289 calories, Protein 2g, Carbohydrate 75g, Fat 0.2g, Saturated fat none, Fibre 3g, Added sugar 59g, Salt 0.02g.*

TIP

The American term 'winter squash' covers all of those members of the cucurbita group which have tough, hard rinds and keep for at least a month or two, often much longer. With a few exceptions, the flesh is yellow to orange. Store until needed in a cool airy place – a dry garage is ideal – but once you've cut the squash, use it straight away even if that means cooking and freezing what you can't eat immediately.

FRANCES BENDIXON'S ULTIMATE PUMPKIN PIE ❋

There are as many recipes for pumpkin pie (the essential American Thanksgiving dessert) as there are people who make it. Although Frances Bendixon's ancestors were among the pilgrims who set sail for New England on the *Mayflower* back in the 17th century, she makes no claims to cooking the authentic pumpkin pie. She cooks the ultimate pumpkin pie. The secret is to use double cream (rather than milk or evaporated milk) and, most importantly, to drain the pumpkin purée overnight. This pie is so rich that it really doesn't need any embellishment. However, if you insist on going right over the top, serve it with whipped cream flavoured with brandy, or a scoop of vanilla ice cream.

Serves 6–8

280g/10oz shortcrust pastry (page 62)

2 large eggs, size 1 or 2

400g/14oz thoroughly drained pumpkin or squash purée (See Tip)

1½ tsp ground cinnamon

½ tsp ground ginger

½ tsp ground allspice

½ tsp salt

250ml/9fl oz double cream

125ml/4fl oz maple syrup or to taste

1   Place a baking sheet in the oven and heat to 220C/425F/Gas 7. Line a deep 23cm/9in pie plate or tart tin with the pastry. Use a fork to decorate the rim. Prick the base with a fork and chill until needed.

2   Beat the eggs, then beat in the pumpkin or squash purée, followed by the spices and salt, then the cream. Add the maple syrup gradually, tasting as you do so. If you used a sweet squash then you may not need all of it. Taste and add extra spices if you think it needs a little more pepping up. Pour the mixture into the pastry case.

3   Place the filled case on the hot baking sheet in the oven. Bake for 10 minutes to start the crust browning, then reduce the heat to 190C/375F/Gas 5. Cook for about 30 minutes or until the filling looks set around the edges and about halfway to the middle of the pie, but the centre is still a bit wobbly. Serve warm or cold.

Nutrition notes per serving for six: *497 calories, Protein 6g, Carbohydrate 40g, Fat 36g, Saturated fat 20g, Fibre 2g, Added sugar 16g, Salt 0.98g.*

❋ *Freeze the pie in its tin for up to 1 month. Defrost thoroughly, then reheat, covered, until piping hot.*

TIP

To prepare pumpkin or squash purée: take a 1.25kg/2¾lb wedge of pumpkin or other winter squash, or three large butternut squashes. Cut in half if necessary, and remove the seeds and fibres in the centre. Place on an oiled baking sheet, cut sides down, cover with foil and bake at 190C/375F/Gas 5 until soft – anything from 40 minutes to 2½ hours! Leave on the sheet until cool enough to handle. Scoop out the pulp and process until smooth, or pass through the fine blade of a mouli-légumes. Tip into a colander lined with split-open coffee filters or a double layer of muslin and leave to drain overnight. This long draining to eliminate any wateriness makes all the difference between take-it-or-leave-it pumpkin pie, and a very more-ish one. It's a trick worth remembering when making other recipes requiring pumpkin purée. Weigh out the amount required. Any leftover pulp can be frozen.

Basic Recipes

SHORTCRUST PASTRY

A versatile pastry which can be used for sweet or savoury dishes.

Makes 350g/12oz

225g/8oz plain flour

pinch of salt

115g/4oz chilled butter, diced

1 egg yolk, beaten

iced water

1   Sift the flour with the salt. Rub the butter into the flour until it resembles fine breadcrumbs. Make a well in the centre and add the egg yolk and enough iced water to form a soft dough – one and a half to two tablespoons should be enough.
2   Mix quickly and lightly and knead very briefly to smooth out. Wrap and chill for at least 30 minutes in the fridge. Bring back to room temperature before using.

VINAIGRETTE

Please don't waste your money on bottles of ready-made French dressing. They are ridiculously expensive and not terribly good either. Making a proper vinaigrette or French dressing is child's play. After that is left over will keep in a screw-top jar in the fridge for several weeks.

Makes enough for a generous 6-person salad

1 tbsp wine vinegar

½ tsp Dijon mustard (optional)

salt and freshly ground black pepper

4–5 tbsp extra virgin olive oil or groundnut oil

1   In a salad bowl, mix the vinegar with the mustard, if using, and the salt and pepper. Whisk in the oil, a tablespoon at a time. After the fourth spoonful taste – if it is on the sharp side, whisk in the last spoonful of oil and more if necessary. Adjust seasoning.
2   Alternatively, place all the ingredients in a screw-top jar, close tightly and shake to mix. Taste and adjust the seasoning or add more oil as necessary.

TOMATO SAUCE

This is a very good, relatively smooth tomato sauce, which makes allowances for the lesser quality of North European tomatoes. Tomato purée and a little sugar compensate to some degree, and so too does generous seasoning.

Makes about 600ml/1 pint

900g/2lb ripe tomatoes (skinned and seeded)

1 large onion, chopped

3 garlic cloves, chopped

3 tbsp olive oil

2 tbsp tomato purée

½–1 tbsp sugar

salt and freshly ground black pepper

3 fresh basil sprigs

1   Liquidize or process the tomatoes. Place the onion, garlic and olive oil in a large pan and cook until the onion is tender. Add the tomatoes, tomato purée, sugar and seasoning and simmer gently for 30 minutes. You can substitute 600ml/1 pint passata (sieved tomatoes) for the processed tomatoes.
2   Add the basil and cook for a further 5–10 minutes. Taste and add a little more sugar if the sauce is on the sharp side. Adjust the seasoning. Remove the basil sprigs before using.

INDEX